# IRISH BUS PHOTOGRAPHERS
# IRISH BUSES
## 2012-2017

**Paul Savage**

D1420105

**COLOURPOINT BOOKS**

Published 2018 by Colourpoint Books
An imprint of Colourpoint Creative Ltd
Colourpoint House, Jubilee Business Park
Jubilee Road, Newtownards, BT23 4YH
Tel: 028 9182 6339
Fax: 028 9182 1900
E-mail: info@colourpoint.co.uk
Web: www.colourpoint.co.uk

First Edition
First Impression

A catalogue record for this book is available from the British Library.

Designed by April Sky Design, Newtownards
Tel: 028 9182 7195 • Web: www.aprilsky.co.uk

Printed by GPS Colour Graphics Ltd, Belfast

ISBN 978-1-78073-178-0

*Front cover:* In 1975, Córas Iompair Éireann created the *Expressway* brand for its express coach services across Ireland.
Forty years on, in February 2015, Bus Éireann re-launched *Expressway* with a striking new red and silver livery.
Volvo B11R/Sunsundegui SC7 VE 2 is seen departing Dublin Airport for Cork on 24 August 2016.

*Rear cover:* When is an Ulsterbus bus not an Ulsterbus bus? When it's a Metro bus, of course! On 10 July 2014, Volvo B10BLE/Wright Renown
No 2776, transferred to Metro (Short Strand depot) in May, heads south towards Forestside shopping centre on a
mid-afternoon service 31 journey via the Castlereagh Road.

# CONTENTS

# INTRODUCTION

Welcome to Vol. 4 in Colourpoint's Irish Bus Photographers series. My previous contribution, Vol. 2 in the series, was very well received, I'm pleased to say, with generous comments and good reviews in the enthusiast press. So, here, three years on, is another selection of bus pictures, this time in a different format, inspired by the two volumes of pictures taken by my good friend Richard Newman on his visits to Ireland, north and south, between 1964 and 1968.

In the late spring of 2017, I began the process of selecting pictures for this volume, restricting myself to the period 2012 to 2017, so roughly fifty years after Richard's visits, and, having set aside for review well over 1000 images, commenced to narrow that number down to something more manageable, a task easier said than done. Having sorted the pictures by operator, I very quickly realised that that would make for a very boring book; it would be laid out in big blocks of Dublin Bus blue and yellow, Bus Éireann red and white, Metro magenta/grey and Ulsterbus blue/grey, with many of the private sector operators using white as a base for their liveries, so what to do? Well, so that the range of colours applied to buses and coaches would be spread throughout the book, I chose to illustrate it by location, making the book effectively a tour north from Dublin via Dundalk, the Mournes, Co Down, Belfast, Co Antrim, the North Coast, Derry~Londonderry and into Co Donegal, finishing with Enniskillen, Armagh, Craigavon and Lisburn, so that the reader might appreciate the variety that could have been seen in the period reviewed and which, indeed, is still there.

Dublin Bus is the main provider of bus services in the city and over half the bus journeys made in Ireland are on its services. Wright Eclipse Gemini-bodied Volvo B9TL VG27 is seen on O'Connell Street.

Dublin Bus route 16 links the airport across the city to Ballinteer in the south by way of Santry, Drumcondra, O'Connell Street, Harold's Cross and Terenure, a journey of about an hour and three-quarters. Here Summerhill Garage-based Volvo B7TL AX549, with Alexander Dennis ALX400 bodywork, is seen at the start of its long journey.

Bus Éireann operates most intercity and local buses outside Dublin. Fleetnumber AM 15, allocated to Dundalk, is an Alexander Dennis Enviro200.

For many visitors to Ireland, their first sight of a bus or coach is at Dublin Airport so I chose that as the starting point for our journey and, as will become obvious, the variety of vehicles to be seen there, and the range of colours they wear, in my humble opinion, well justifies the decision to set out this volume as we have. Similarly, the overview of operations in Dublin city centre shows the variety of chassis and body types which could, and can, be seen in this vibrant, modern city. Space constraints meant that a look beyond the city's central area wasn't something that could be considered, but certainly, most classes of Bus Éireann and Dublin Bus vehicles can be seen there anyway, with variety added by the colours and vehicle types of the sightseeing operators. And what city would be complete without a former London Transport AEC Routemaster available for sightseeing duty?

Richard's visits reached further south in the Republic of Ireland so I apologise for the lack of pictures south and west of Dublin, but my intention was to give a flavour of what can/could be seen. One place not visited by Richard was Dundalk and the Co Louth town still provides much variety for the visiting enthusiast, with buses, including double-deckers, from Bus Éireann, Halpenny Transport, also with double-deckers on the town service and its almost one-hundred-year-old route to the seaside village of Blackrock, and Matthews of Inniskeen, Co Monaghan with its modern coach fleet on a frequent express service to Dublin.

Moving north, we arrive at Newry and the first sightings of the ocean blue and grey livery applied to most buses in the Ulsterbus fleet. Bus Éireann and Halpenny vehicles can be seen here too, on their respective cross-border services

to Dundalk. Crossing the scenic Mourne range brings us to the sea at Newcastle before continuing, eventually, to Bangor. Perhaps unfortunately, this section provides little in the way of anything other than Ulsterbus blue and grey so I've chosen to illustrate it with locations perhaps not at the top of the tourist itinerary.

Belfast has changed much in recent years and the number of visitors is astonishing. Indeed, it is now an important call on cruise ship itineraries, with over 80 visits in 2017 and expected to be much higher in 2018. These calls provide work for the coaching operators in the independent sector, allowing them to invest in new, or at least newer, vehicles for their fleets, providing more colour and variety for the enthusiast. Of course, the predominant colour in Belfast city centre is the magenta of the Citybus (Metro) fleet, though September 2018 will bring the purple of the Van Hool Exqui.City bus rapid

transit vehicles on the Glider east–west cross-city route.

The Giant's Causeway, on the north coast of Northern Ireland, is a big tourist draw and worth a visit anytime, but, for the enthusiast, particularly on a day when one of the larger cruise ships is docked at Belfast – and even better if that day happens to be a summer Saturday! The improvements to the road networks north and south mean that Dublin to the Causeway day trips are now a practical proposition and several operators have added such to their offerings.

The city of Londonderry – the official title – or Derry, as many refer to it, is the second city of Northern Ireland and is situated just a few miles from the border with Co Donegal, drawing much business and many visitors from that county. The change in attitudes in Northern Ireland following the Belfast Agreement has seen Derry~Londonderry prosper and it's now a popular stopping-off place for coach parties on

*Opposite top left:* Halpenny Transport, of Blackrock, can trace its ancestry back almost one hundred years, to The Violet bus company which was founded in 1920, and has operated the route between seaside Blackrock and Dundalk since. It has, from the 1930s, purchased many of its service buses from the state-owned operators in Northern Ireland and its January 2016 acquisition was no exception. This Scania L94UB, with Wright Solar bodywork, came from Ulsterbus where it had been numbered 734, both of which facts are obvious in this view from 6 February 2016, by which time it had been registered locally as 01 LH 11129.

*Opposite top right:* Dublin Coach Mercedes-Benz Tourismo 171 KE 1403 arrives at Glengall Street, Belfast on 24 March 2017, the second day of operation of route 400.

*Right:* Belfast city services are provided by (magenta) Citybus (t/a Metro), while out-of-town services are run by (blue) Ulsterbus. Occasional inter-company transfers can see sights like blue Volvo B10BLE No 2776 running on Metro routes.

tours to scenic Co Donegal. In August 2017, the Ulsterbus city services were branded Foyle Metro, with a new burnt orange colour applied to the city fleet, which was also upgraded with the allocation of 16 new Optare Versa V1170s. Buses and coaches from Bus Éireann, McGonagle's (Buncrana), Reddin's (Muff) and North West Busways (Clar, Redcastle) can be seen around the city on schools services and cross-border bus and coach routes.

Crossing the border, we stop off at Letterkenny, the largest town in Co Donegal, before heading back into Northern Ireland at Strabane and on to Omagh. After some time at Enniskillen to view the variety there, it's along the Clogher Valley to Dungannon, then the cathedral city of Armagh and on to our final stop at Lisburn via calls at Craigavon and Lurgan.

I do hope you enjoy the selection of pictures in the book and approve of how it's been designed. Thank you to Malcolm Johnston and the team at Colourpoint Books for making my images and text so presentable and to Jonathan McDonnell and Noel O'Rawe for casting a critical eye during the various stages of production.

*Paul Savage*
*Belfast*
*September 2018*

# DUBLIN AIRPORT

The first sight of a bus or coach for many visitors to Ireland will be at Dublin Airport, which is located about ten miles north of the city centre. The national, state-owned operator, Bus Éireann, operates services to the airport from most major centres. Here we see its fleetnumber SE 50, a Scania K410EB6 with Irizar i6 coachwork new in 2016, leaving the airport for Dublin city centre on its journey from Sligo. Bus Éireann is required to use bi-lingual destination displays, the Irish being shown here.

*Left:* The airport is also served from Northern Ireland by the state-owned operator there, Ulsterbus. Services X1 and X2a run from Belfast while X3 and X4 start at Derry~Londonderry. Ulsterbus No 2053 is a Scania K400EB6/Irizar i6 new in February 2013 and based at Belfast's Great Victoria Street depot.

*Below:* Callinan's of Claregalway operates a mix of stopping and express services between the airport and Galway under the *Citylink* banner. Here Van Hool TX15 Alicron 131 G 2079 starts its journey west on 24 August 2016.

*Top:* Bus Éireann also serves Galway from Dublin Airport with journeys on its services 20 and X20. On the same day as the previous view, Eurolines-liveried Scania K114EB, with Irizar PB coachwork, SP 87 is seen Galway-bound on the airport's Corballis Road South.

*Centre:* At the same location, SP 94, a similarly-bodied Scania K340, repainted to the 2015 *Expressway* livery, passes through en route to its city centre terminus at Busáras, the central bus station, on its long trip from Letterkenny in Co Donegal.

*Bottom:* A fast service between Dublin Airport and Cork is provided by GoBÉ, a joint venture between Bus Éireann and Cummer Coaches (Burke), Tuam, on which the usual vehicles are modern Volvo 9700 coaches, like 151 G 1211. Cummer Coaches, t/a GoBus, operates to Galway in its own right, while Aircoach also provides a fast service between the airport and Cork.

*Left:* Competition on the Letterkenny route is provided by John McGinley, Gortahork, often using one of his Jonckheere-bodied Volvo B11R coaches acquired new in 2014. Here 141 DL 1526 is on Corballis Road South en route to Parnell Square in the city centre.

*Below:* Despite being built at Ballymena, Co Antrim, the Wright StreetLite, in any of its forms, was not, until 2018, a common sight in Ireland, though FirstGroup subsidiary Last Passive (t/a Aircoach) operated one on airport staff shuttle duties. Transferred in from Great Britain, fleetnumber B84 or 11084, now registered 131 D 28391, was PO13 FWR when it worked in England.

*Left:* Last Passive also operates car park shuttle services at the airport using a fleet of Mercedes-Benz Citaro O530G bendybuses such as fleetnumber 11083 (09 D 5303), which was new in January 2009.

*Below:* Dublin Coach, too, provides vehicles for parking shuttles around the airport and, like Last Passive, uses Mercedes-Benz Citaro O530G bendybuses, though in a brighter green livery.

Back now towards the coach station and main bus stops we see Bus Éireann Volvo B12B/Caetano Enigma VC 325 departing on route 30 to Cavan. Other journeys on route 30 extend beyond Cavan to Enniskillen and Donegal Town. When new in August 2003, VC 325 would have worn a mainly white livery, but thirteen years on it had received the then current main fleet livery.

Bus Éireann has revised its livery over the past few years by removing the orange swoops and including more white to the rear of vehicles, as can be seen on 2016 delivery VDL Synergy LD 321 departing on route 133 to Wicklow.

# DUBLIN CITY CENTRE

Our look proper at buses and coaches in the city centre begins around the corner from Heuston station, by the gates to the city's famous Phoenix Park, which at 1,750 acres makes it one of the largest such sites in any European capital city and contains Dublin Zoo, the Papal Cross, erected for the visit of Pope John Paul II on 29 September 1979, and Áras an Uachtaráin, the residence of the President of Ireland. Here, on Conyngham Road, on 24 August 2016, is East Lancs-bodied Volvo B7TL 05 D 13455, new in 2005, from the fleet of Dualway, Rathcoole.

Frequent, hop-on, hop-off city tours are also offered by the city's main bus service provider, Dublin Bus, whose metallic green and yellow-liveried Volvo B7TL/Alexander Dennis ALX400 AX511, new in August 2006, is seen on the park's Chesterfield Avenue. The livery worn by AX511 was replaced in 2017 with a lighter green scheme and *Do Dublin* branding (see pages 22 and 30).

Dualway uses similar vehicles in its fleet, including the former Dublin Bus AV35, with a tidy, but perhaps not so stylish conversion to open-top layout.

Open-top city tours are also offered by Dublin Coach using gold Cityscape-branded Plaxton President-bodied Dennis Tridents acquired from Metroline, London. Some have been converted to full open-top layout, while others, such as 03 KE 16279, retain the roof in the first two bays.

Our next stop is on Victoria Quay, by the famous St James's Gate Brewery, home of Guinness, where we see Volvo B10M-62/Plaxton Excalibur 99 MH 15067 from the fleet of Carolan, Nobber laying-over between runs on commuter service 191. This vehicle was new to Ulsterbus in 1999 as its No 1635 (BCZ 1635) and spent its entire service at Coleraine, much of it as the depot tour coach. It was last noted working for Eamon McDaid at Ballymagan, Buncrana, Co Donegal.

At Heuston station, departing on the long run south-east to Ballywaltrim on route 145, is Dublin Bus tri-axle Volvo B9TL VT30. The bodywork is Alexander Dennis's Enviro500 model and the buses in the 2007 batch each seat 93 passengers.

*Top left:* Route 145 would take us along the quays by the River Liffey to O'Connell Bridge and the city centre proper. Here Dublin Bus SG1, its first Volvo B5TL/Wright Gemini 3, crosses from Burgh Quay to Aston Quay on its way west to the Blanchardstown shopping centre.

*Top right:* Crossing O'Connell Bridge by open-top bus gives good views along the Liffey, from the port in the east towards Heuston Station in the west. However, on 1 December 2012, there weren't many customers onboard Dualway's Alexander-bodied Volvo Olympian 98 D 77635 availing of the opportunity. This vehicle was new to London United.

*Left:* 2016 was a year of commemoration in Ireland, with many events and exhibitions marking the Easter Rising of 1916. Dublin Bus operated a special sightseeing tour using Volvo B7TL/ Alexander Dennis ALX400 AX544, the livery featuring street scenes and a large image of a Dublin tram.

*Top left:* Bought new in 2007, Dualway's East Lancs Visionaire-bodied Volvo B9TL 07 D 29 runs on to O'Connell Bridge on 24 August 2016.

*Top right:* As we head north on O'Connell Street, Bus Éireann Volvo B9TL/Wright Eclipse Gemini 2 VWD 18 turns in to Lower Abbey Street as it nears the end of its journey from Ashbourne on 15 April 2017. VWD 18 was transferred from Broadstone garage to Drogheda in October 2017.

*Left:* VWD 18 was displaced from Dublin's Broadstone garage by the arrival of a batch of long wheelbase Volvo B5TLs with Wright Gemini 3 bodies, like VWD 77 seen here on 29 August 2017 at the same location.

19 October 2013 was a wet day in Dublin, which likely accounts for the few passengers, all under cover, onboard Dualway's Plaxton President-bodied Volvo B7TL 03 D 82308, another import from the United Kingdom.

At the end of Volvo B9TL production, Volvo had 20 chassis fitted with Wright Eclipse Gemini 2 bodies built as stock vehicles. Dualway purchased three and had them converted by Wrights to part open-top layout. 151 D 26628 is shown here on the wide thoroughfare of O'Connell Street on 25 March 2017.

*Above:* A few weeks later, at just about the same spot, Bernard Kavanagh's tri-axle Mercedes-Benz Tourismo 161 D 10183 is seen on a city sightseeing tour for a party of visitors travelling with CIÉ Tours International. In years past, coaching for such tours was provided by CIÉ then Bus Éireann, but now it's all contracted to the private sector.

*Left:* Dublin Mini Coaches also got in on the 1916 Rising commemorations with a Rise of The Rebels bus tour for which former Dublin Bus Volvo B7TL AV160 was specially fitted-out as a building under siege. The tour also operated in 2017, as shown here when AV160 was captured on O'Connell Street on 28 October. A quick look at the front registration plate might suggest the bus dates from 2008, but it was actually new in 2000.

*Right:* Dublin Bus head office is located on O'Connell Street, as can be seen in this October 2013 view of Alexander (Belfast) RH-bodied Leyland Olympian RH87, new in April 1991. After a period on driver training work, it was converted to open-top for city tour duty, by Louth Commercials, in the late summer of 2003.

*Below left:* In 2017, the Dublin Bus city tours fleet received an upgrade with the conversion to part open-top layout of three Volvo B9TL/Alexander Dennis Enviro400s, these being EV21 (*illustrated*), 49 and 50.

*Below right:* Dualway also upgraded its fleet in 2017 with the purchase of a Volvo B5TL with Wright Gemini 3 part open-top bodywork similar in specification to those supplied to Lothian and Stagecoach in the United Kingdom.

And what sightseeing operation would be complete without a former London Transport AEC Routemaster? Cityscape No 752 is the former RM316 and looks very smart in its gold livery as it heads north on O'Connell Street before circuiting Parnell Square. The tracks in the foreground are the LUAS extension to Broombridge, which weren't in use at the date of this view (29 August 2017), opening to passengers on 9 December.

Surrounded by works associated with the LUAS tram extension to Broombridge, Dublin Bus Volvo B9TL/Wright Eclipse Gemini GT135, new in October 2013, turns into Parnell Square West on a route 140 journey to IKEA. The GT class reintroduced the dual door layout on new deliveries to the main Dublin Bus fleet after a gap of thirteen years, the last vehicles with this arrangement being 15 Alexander ALX400-bodied Volvo B7TLs delivered in 2000 for the airport service. Dublin Bus specifies a more raked back windscreen on its Wright Gemini deliveries, which results in a peak at the top of the screen; this arrangement is to help reduce interior reflection at night.

On the diagonally opposite side of the square now is Bus Éireann SC 331, a 12.4m Scania K320EB4 with coachwork to Irizar's Century design. When photographed, it was working on Dublin area commuter routes and was based at the city's Broadstone garage. It has since been transferred to Co Donegal where it can be found on local service routes. The revised livery, without orange, was introduced on this batch of coaches.

The Easter Rising of 1916 was also remembered on a
Bus Éireann vehicle. VWD 22, a Volvo B5TL with Wright
Gemini 3 bodywork, new in 2015, was chosen to
highlight the role of women in the Rising.

*Top left:* In just about the same spot is similar VWD 24, which wears the livery variation introduced in 2015, which removed orange from the colour scheme.

*Top right:* Matthews of Inniskeen, Co Monaghan, operates express and commuter services into Dublin from the Dundalk and Drogheda areas using a mix of modern Scania and Volvo coaches like 141 MN 362, a Scania K360/Irizar Century, pictured on Parnell Square East arriving on the noon departure from Grange Rath via Bettystown, Laytown and Julianstown.

*Left:* In addition to its fleet of Berkhof-bodied double-deck coaches, Bus Éireann also ran 49 VDL SB2000/Berkhof coaches, like LC 215 crossing Cathal Brugha Street on 24 August 2016, when about eight and a half years old.

At the date of this photograph – 28 October 2017 – Dublin Bus was operating more than 300 of the Volvo B5TL model, but by the year's end that number had increased to almost 370. SG312, seen loading at stop No 4725 on O'Connell Street en route to Bride's Glen, was then a recent delivery.

Southbound now on O'Connell Street and Dublin Bus Volvo B9TL/Alexander Dennis Enviro400 EV46 turns from Cathal Brugha Street on a route 123 journey to Kilnamanagh Road, a route once operated with *CityImp*-branded mini- and midibuses.

Showing a good coating of winter road dirt in this 2 January 2015 view, Dublin Bus Volvo B7TL/Alexander ALX400 AV123, working on cross-city route 16 between the airport and Ballinteer, was one of just 15 of the 648 similar buses delivered, to be built to dual-door layout, for use on the airport express service.

Illustrating a livery variation now gone from the fleet, Dublin Bus Volvo B7TL/Alexander Dennis ALX400 AX531 heads out to Sandymount on cross-city route 1. This livery variation survived from the days when Dublin Bus frequently provided buses for wedding hires.

To the Custom House Quay now. Mention has already been made of the fast service options between Dublin Airport, the city centre and Cork, using the motorway network. The GoBÉ option was illustrated at the airport, so here's the Aircoach offering from 1 December 2012. The coach is No C74, a Scania K340EB4 with Caetano Levante body built in Portugal. It was previously No 23504 in the First Cymru fleet, registered FJ56 PFN.

A view now, from 15 April 2017, of Dublin Bus AX510, one of the fleet of Volvo B7TL sightseeing buses, on O'Connell Bridge. It had not long since been painted from the metallic green and yellow *Dublin Bus Tour* scheme to the lighter green *Do Dublin* version, now applied to the tours fleet.

*Left:* Seen on O'Connell Bridge on 24 August 2016 when operating a journey on route 760 to Park West is Express Bus 99 C 18899, a Volvo B10L, with Liberator bodywork built by Wrights. This vehicle was new in June 1999 as Bus Éireann fleetnumber VWL 10.

*Below left:* JJ Kavanagh & Sons, Urlingford, Co Kilkenny, is a well-respected operator of high-quality coaches, both on tours and express work. Engaged on the latter on 15 April 2017 was Mercedes-Benz Tourismo 171 KK 1, then less than four months old. It's heading for Clonmel on the 13:30 route 717.

*Below right:* Route 817, which provides a once-a-day link between Kilkenny and Dublin, is operated by Bernard Kavanagh, Urlingford, under contract to Transport for Ireland. Volvo B12B/Plaxton Panther 06 KK 8173, new to Park's of Hamilton as LSK 509, carries TfI livery, appropriately branded.

Moving on to College Street and Dublin Bus AV367, yet another of the 648 ALX400-bodied Volvo B7TLs. In this August 2017 view, it's heading west on peak-hour route 66X to Captain's Hill, Maynooth.

Not another Volvo, but one of the ten TransBus-bodied TransBus Tridents purchased by Dublin Bus in July 2003; you might notice differences in the window layout and spacing. This is fleetnumber DT4, based at Harristown, and working on peak-hour route 41X to Swords and Knocksedan via the Port Tunnel. The final runs by the DT class were undertaken in December 2017.

Eirebus's *Fingal Express* division operates services to the northern outer suburbs, such as Skerries and Lusk. Running to the former is MAN 18.400/Farebus Califa 10 D 12299, a model rare anywhere in Ireland or the United Kingdom.

Most Bus Éireann *Expressway* and many of its local services depart from Busáras and surrounding streets. Occasionally, maybe more frequently, journeys are contracted out to operators in the private sector, including on 6 January 2018 when Bruen of Coolock provided Volvo B7TL/Alexander Dennis ALX400 03 D 121448 for the 15:20 route 103 journey from Beresford Place to Ratoath via Ashbourne. The red livery and roundel on the front show this bus had previously been in service in London, with Arriva as its fleetnumber VLA26.

On 29 August 2017, the 18:15 Busáras to Kells was contracted to Maynooth-based James Mullally Coach Hire who supplied Volvo B7TL/East Lancs Myllennium Vyking 04 KE 16467, previously registered PG04 WJA (fleetnumber VLE20) in the London United fleet.

The newest coaches in Bus Éireann's fleet are the members of the LC class numbered 301 upwards. They are VDL Futura FHD2 models and feature wheelchair lifts towards the rear on the nearside. LC 327 was captured on Amiens Street on 1 July 2017 as it headed for Talbot Street to await its next turn on route 101 to Drogheda.

Before we leave the city and head north, here are two views of types which no longer feature in the Dublin Bus fleet. On 24 November 2012, Dublin Bus very kindly provided to members of Irish Transport Heritage for a farewell tour, Volvo Olympian/ Alexander 'RH' RV 606, seen here near the Stocking Avenue terminus.

1 July 2017 saw a farewell tour organised by some Dublin-based enthusiasts for the DT class Dennis Tridents. DT2 was the allocated bus, seen here at Bulfin Road, in the Inchicore district.

# DUNDALK

Our journey north is broken at Dundalk, about ten miles from the border with Northern Ireland. Dublin is linked to Dundalk by train, Bus Éireann route 100X and services 900 and 901 operated by Matthews, Inniskeen, Co. Monaghan. Here, on Dublin Street, is Bus Éireann Volvo B11R/Sunsundegui SC7 fleetnumber VE 9, a few minutes into its journey south on the 12:30 motorway express 100X departure on 27 February 2016.

*Top left:* Matthews' services depart from The Marshes shopping centre and are operated with a fleet of luxury coaches, many bought new, but with judicious pre-owned purchases too. 09 KE 928 is Volvo B12B(T) with one of the first examples of the Plaxton Elite body and was displayed at Euro Bus Expo in 2008.

*Top right:* Matthews also operates services to concerts and sporting events at various venues, such as the Aviva Stadium in Dublin, as displayed on the front of Ayats Bravo 1 double-decker 10 G 5274 departing The Marshes on 18 March 2017. This vehicle had worked for Jim Burke's Cummer Coaches, Tuam, before arriving with Matthews.

*Left:* In August 2016, Matthews acquired four Volvo B13RT/Plaxton Panther 70-seater coaches which had previously worked for Scottish operator Park's of Hamilton. 11 MN 2628 was registered SG11 ZYB *(LSK 879)* when it worked in Great Britain.

By summer 2016, the latest addition to the Halpenny service bus fleet was Volvo B7TL/Alexander ALX400 01 D 10221, which had been Dublin Bus AV221 in its previous life. It arrived at Blackrock in July, was repainted in the company's blue/yellow livery and entered service in August. In this view, taken on 7 October 2017 at the junction of Market Square, Clanbrassil Street and Crowe Street, it was returning from a town service run and would shortly arrive at the town centre stop at Roden Place.

The Halpenny Transport service to Blackrock, and The Violet before it, departs from a stand on Roden Place. On 7 October 2017, Scania L94UB 01 LH 11129, looking very smart in fleet blue and yellow livery, has just arrived with the 12:30 departure from Newry and will leave again shortly as the 13:00 to the seaside village of Blackrock.

*Top left:* Passing through Market Square on 11 November 2017, working a journey on town service 174 between the bus station on Long Walk and Muirhevnamuir, is Bus Éireann Alexander Dennis Enviro200 AM 15, one of 19 similar vehicles in the fleet. The bus station on Market Square, in use since Great Northern Railway days, was relocated to the Long Walk in 1985, the current building opening in Spring 1999, though the official opening was delayed until 17 September that year to coincide with the opening of a new Ulsterbus station at Armagh.

*Top right:* Dundalk garage frequently turns out two of its double-deck allocation of three on town services duties. In this February 2016 view, Volvo B7TL/East Lancs Myllennium Vyking DD 24 performs a duty on the Bay Estate route. It has just entered Roden Place, where St Patrick's Cathedral is behind the photographer.

*Left:* 2016 saw Dundalk garage receive from Cork a pair of Wright Eclipse 2-bodied Volvo B7RLE low floor single-deckers, VWL 301/2. On 21 May, VWL 301 was photographed on Long Walk having just left the bus station on a run to Muirhevnamuir. 2017 saw similar, but older (2008), vehicles transfer in from Limerick garage.

26 November 2016, and Volvo B7TL/East Lancs Myllennium Vyking DD 13, looking very much in need of a run through the bus wash, has arrived at Dundalk bus station on route 167 from Ardee. DD 13, new in January 2002, was the oldest of the three similar vehicles then allocated to Dundalk; DD24/8 were exactly two years newer. They were replaced in 2017 by the transfer of Volvo B9TL/Wright Eclipse Gemini VWD 1/2 from Galway and similar, but Eclipse Gemini 2-bodied, VWD 17 from Broadstone.

Several of these Volvo B7Ls, with Wright Eclipse Urban low floor bodies, arrived at Dundalk, from Cork, in 2016 and saw service across the route network operated there. The body was designed specifically for city or town service use, with a low flat floor almost the full length of the saloon, so the appearance of VWL 133 on town service route 174 to Fatima on 7 October 2017 was a most appropriate allocation.

The three DD class Volvo B7TL/East Lancs Myllennium Vyking double-deckers allocated to Dundalk were replaced in October 2017 with three, newer, Wright-bodied Volvo B9TLs – VWD 1, 2 and 17, the first two transferred from Galway and the last from Broadstone (Dublin). Eclipse Gemini-bodied VWD 2 leans into the turn out of the bus station as it departs on the 13:30 town service to Fatima on 11 November 2017. VWD 17, which carries an Eclipse Gemini 2 body, had just departed for Muirhevnamuir and can be glimpsed in the background.

## COUNTY DOWN

We cross the Louth/Armagh border now and arrive in Northern Ireland at Forkhill, Co Armagh, where Ulsterbus Optare Solo M920SL No 1910 was photographed on 5 July 2014 when working service 443, the seasonal *Slieve Gullion* Rambler. The 443 served Camlough, Mullaghbawn, Forkhill, Slieve Gullion Forest Park and Meigh on a scenic circular route from Newry.

*Right:* To Newry City now and the Buttercrane Quay, the departure point for Halpenny Transport's service to Dundalk on which Optare Solo M850 03 LH 11246 is seen in this Spring 2016 view. This bus is another acquired from Ulsterbus where it had been No 1870 (SCZ 3870). It was sold in 2017 to Manning's, Limerick. Near this point on the quay, the Great Northern Railway's line between Newry (Edward Street) and Warrenpoint crossed the Newry Canal by way of a sliding bridge, some remains of which can still be seen.

*Below:* There are several options for passengers travelling between the Dundalk area and Newry. There's the Enterprise rail service, operated jointly by Northern Ireland Railways and Irish Rail, Halpenny Transport's direct service via Killeen and Bus Éireann services 160 via Ravensdale and Killeen and 161 via Greenore, Carlingford and Omeath, on which Scania K114EB/Irizar PB SP 3 is seen passing the Buttercrane shopping centre. SP 3 was new in August 2005.

The bus station at Newry is convenient for the city centre and is unusual in that it is built on an island, Sugar Island to be precise, with the canal to one side and the Newry River to the other. The station building sits over the river, linking to The Mall. Here we see Ulsterbus No 515, a Volvo B7RLE with Alexander Dennis Enviro300 Rural bodywork, arriving on the coastal route from Kilkeel.

13:15 on 1 August 2015 and Bus Éireann Volvo B12B/Sunsundegui Sideral VG 3 heads for home at Dundalk on service 160. The VG class comprised 20 similar vehicles, which were all withdrawn and sold in 2015.

The 13:30 departure on Bus Éireann service 161 to Dundalk via Carlingford on the same day was Alexander Dennis Enviro200 AM 104, one of a pair of similar vehicles then allocated to Dundalk garage; there were just four in the fleet, the other two being at Waterford. Following the coasts of Carlingford Lough and Dundalk Bay, AM 104 would reach Dundalk about 14:50.

The X1 express coach service between Belfast and Dublin calls at Sprucefield, Banbridge and Newry and is jointly operated by Bus Éireann and Ulsterbus. On 5 July 2014, the noon departure from Belfast leaves Newry at 13:00, a few minutes late. The coach is Bus Éireann Scania K340EB/Irizar PB SP 110, which is fitted with a side-mounted wheelchair lift. When new in 2008, SP 110 was allocated to CIÉ Tours International duties.

*Top:* The largest vehicles operating on the X1 service are the four VDL Synergy double-deck coaches provided by Bus Éireann and which comfortably seat 81 passengers. LE 1, new in 2012, leaves Newry for Dublin Airport and Dublin city centre on 1 August 2015, by which date it had received the last version of the company's Expressway livery.

*Left:* At the same spot, just where the exit from the bus station crosses the canal to join the quays, is Ulsterbus Volvo B7R/Wright High Capacity No 180, one of 220 similar vehicles in the fleet. No 180 is understood to have been from an order placed by a local private sector operator, which was subsequently cancelled. Allocated to Newry, No 180 has spent much of its life working from the outstation at Crossmaglen.

We leave Newry now and head east across the Mourne Mountains towards the seaside town of Newcastle. En route, we see Ulsterbus Scania L94UB No 705, crossing the tight Dunnywater Bridge over the Annalong River. It's 15 August 2015 and No 705 was performing a turn on *Mourne Rambler* service 405, which links Newcastle with Spelga Dam, the Silent Valley reservoir and numerous walking trails in this scenic area. No 705 was fitted out for the carriage of a small number of bicycles.

Each August, the local council organises the Festival of Flight at Newcastle, which requires the provision of extra buses on service 520 from Belfast as well as a large park-and-ride operation. The extra buses are often drawn from the Metro fleet in Belfast and in 2017 one of those was relatively new Volvo B5TL/ Wright Gemini 3 No 2121, seen here arriving in the town centre from the park-and-ride site off the Castlewellan road.

On now in 2017 to where the Mountains of Mourne sweep down to the sea and Ulsterbus Volvo B7TL/Alexander No 2935 arriving at Newcastle from Kilkeel, with a backdrop of Slieve Donard. No 2935 was new in the Spring of 2001, but didn't enter service until October, by which time it had been allocated to Ulsterbus rather than the intended Citybus. After six years, it reached its intended home, but was transferred back to Ulsterbus in November 2014.

*Right:* We continue north and east to arrive at Ballylucas, the terminus of service 16d from Downpatrick. I suspect this service may date from 1950 and the closure by the Ulster Transport Authority of the entire County Down section of railway lines, with the exception of Bangor. On 15 August 2015, Ulsterbus Scania K230UB/Wright Solar Rural No 442 waits time prior to its short run back to Downpatrick. En route it will pass the railway station at Ballynoe, still in use as a private dwelling.

*Below:* It's not just at Ballynoe where the railway station remains, though here at Ardglass it is derelict. Ulsterbus maintains a small outstation of four vehicles at this fishing port and the allocation on 30 July 2016 consisted of Scania K230UB/Wright Solar Rural Nos 407 and 442, also Volvo B7R/Wright SchoolRun Nos 195 and 196. The building beyond was previously the bus garage.

*Left:* On along the Co Down coast to Ballyhornan where, on the same day, the much-delayed 13:40 service 16a to Downpatrick via Ardglass and Killough, operated by Volvo B9TL/Wright Eclipse Gemini No 2236, loads its last few passengers at 14:05.

*Below:* Passing through Kilclief, the next village is Strangford, where the A2 road, which follows the coast from Newry to Derry~Londonderry, gets a bit wet as it crosses the narrows to Portaferry on Transport NI's two modern passenger and vehicle ferries. Strangford is the terminus of service 16e from Downpatrick and on 19 September 2015 Ulsterbus Optare Solo M920SL No 1902 is waiting time to return to the county town. No 1902 now works for Stena Line at Belfast Harbour.

We remain on the western side on Strangford Lough for this view of Ulsterbus Volvo B7TL/Alexander Dennis ALX400 No 2992 passing Killlyleagh Castle, a few minutes into its journey from Shrigley to Belfast via Comber. No 2992 was working from Great Victoria Street depot on Saturday 30 July 2016.

Further west, on the road between Belfast and Newcastle, is Ballynahinch, where there is an outstation of Newcastle depot on the site of the former railway station, just to the left of this view; the allocation is about 20 buses. On 19 August 2014, Newcastle depot's Volvo B9TL/Wright Eclipse Gemini No 2293, then about six-and-a-half years old, heads for Belfast.

Ballynahinch is at one end of service 5b, the other being at Newtownards though, oddly, no journeys operate from one end to the other! Parked on the lay-by at Newtownards bus station is Volvo B7TL/Alexander ALX400 No 2946. The observant reader will have noted that, in 2016, the signage still displayed the Ulsterbus symbol introduced in 1968 and the name style introduced in 1990. No 2946 had transferred from Metro in September 2015.

As part of the Ulsterbus fleet renewal programme, in 2017 Newtownards depot received three new Optare Solo M925SR midibuses, which featured the allover ocean blue livery, also USB power points at each seat. No 1964 has just left the shopping centre en route to the town centre and Castlebawn (Tesco).

We move out to the North Down coast now, to Groomsport, where on 12 July 2014, Belfast Bus Company's Volvo B10M-62/Plaxton Excalibur was parked up during a private hire duty. New to Ulsterbus in 1999 as its No 1645, it was sold in 2013 to Glenferry (Kearney's), Little Island, Co Cork, who passed it on in October that year to Belfast Bus. Much, much earlier, in 1689, the Duke of Schomberg landed his force here on his way to join with King William at the Battle of the Boyne.

*Above:* About three miles west is the town of Bangor, now very much a commuter satellite for Belfast. Seen in this February 2017 view setting down by the Church of Ireland building on Hamilton Road after a trip to Ashbury and Kilmaine is Ulsterbus Scania L94UB/Wright Solar No 2462, which carries a registration number transferred in 2007 from a Leyland Tiger.

*Left:* A feature of the era when Ted Hesketh was Managing Director/Chief Executive was the construction of quality bus and rail stations, that at Bangor being a good example. Here, on 6 May 2017, Optare Solo M920SL No 1900 departs on the 11:55 service 3 along the coast to Donaghadee via Groomsport.

# BELFAST

To Belfast, Northern Ireland's capital city now. Our journey north from Dublin could've been made directly and, from March 2017, very conveniently on a new, non-stop express coach service introduced by Co Kildare-based Dublin Coach using five brand new tri-axle Mercedes-Benz Tourismo coaches such as 171 KE 1400 seen on Belfast's Grosvenor Road, close to its terminus at Glengall Street.

We could also have used the joint Bus Éireann/Ulsterbus X1 service. The eight members of Bus Éireann's LE class VDL Synergy double-deckers were new in 2012. LE 1 was illustrated previously at Newry, but here we see it departing Belfast's Europa Bus Centre when brand new and in its original livery. This area is to be redeveloped with a new transport hub located beyond the bridge in the background.

FirstGroup's Last Passive subsidiary operates in the Republic of Ireland and uses the Aircoach brand for its express services based in Dublin Airport. On 14 July 2012, Kassböhrer Setra S415HD No C30 (24030 in the FirstGroup numbering system), wearing a promotional advert for Northern Ireland events, departs Belfast.

An unusual Aircoach vehicle which appeared in Belfast on several days in May 2012 was this pre-production Volvo B11R with Caetano Levante coachwork, a combination more associated with National Express operations in Great Britain. It's seen turning into Glengall Street and will shortly arrive at its stop outside the Europa Bus Centre.

As mentioned previously the Europa Bus Centre site and the adjacent Great Victoria Street railway station are to be redeveloped by 2023 as an integrated transport hub, which could see the Boyne Bridge, on which the photographer was standing, demolished. On 27 June 2014, Citybus (Metro) Mercedes-Benz O405N No 2102, recently transferred from Ulsterbus, performs a run on service 650 to the park-and-ride site at Black's Road, adjacent to the M1 motorway.

Another view from the bridge shows Ulsterbus MAN ND363F/Ayats Bravo 1 No 2018 on the 14:15 service 261 to Dungannon on 24 February 2017, just about a week after it was re-registered from AXI 318 to FGZ 2244.

31 August 2015 saw the withdrawal from Ulsterbus of some of its most popular buses, these being the Volvo B10BLE/Wright Renowns delivered in 1999/2000. Possibly the last to operate out of Belfast was Craigavon depot's No 2828, seen here on the 16:30 service 51 back to its home depot.

Early August 2017 saw Northern Ireland host the UEFA Women's Under-19 football championship. Team coaches were provided by Ulsterbus, using four Scania K320/Irizar i4 Goldliners and four Scania K360/Irizar i6 coaches from the Tours fleet. One of the latter, No 141, pictured here, was the team coach for the Netherlands.

The Scania K230UB/Wright Solar Rural buses allocated to the Belfast International Airport service since new in 2011 had accumulated substantial mileages and were replaced in late Spring/early Summer 2017 with a batch of ten, long wheelbase Volvo B5TLs with high specification Wright Gemini 3 bodywork, which features leather seats and 4G WiFi. No 2100 is shown turning into Glengall Street, by the Europa Bus Centre.

*Below:* We now take a look round Belfast city centre, calling first at Durham Street where, on 29 July 2016, we see Ulsterbus Scania K410UB/Caetano Invictus No 2030 arriving on the frequent service 212 from Derry~Londonderry. It's passing the former Christ Church, now a suite of classrooms for the Royal Belfast Academical Institution.

*Right:* This Plaxton Paragon-bodied coach belongs to Agnew, Lurgan, and is an example of the relatively rare Dennis R420 chassis. YLZ 202 was new in March 2005 and acquired in October 2013, having previously operated for Anderson, Lochgilphead.

*Top left:* Volvo B12B/Plaxton Panther KEZ 9123 featured in Vol. 2 of this series, photographed at Stranraer on 19 November 2011, the penultimate day of ferry operations at the Galloway port. Then it was an Ulsterbus vehicle, but five years later it was sold to Eurocoach, Bush, Dungannon, where it was converted from a 49-seater to a 70-seater. This view was taken at the Albert Street coach park on 5 December 2017.

*Top right:* The business of Eamonn Rooney, Hilltown, Co Down, includes a lot of school work, not just in his home area but also in Belfast. Several Alexander PS-bodied Volvo B10M-55s were acquired for such work, including R785 DHB, seen at the Albert Street coach parking bays on 4 October 2016.

*Left:* Rooney's also runs a commuter express service to Belfast from Hilltown, Rostrevor, Warrenpoint and Newry using a fleet of smart, white-livered coaches. A rare model anywhere in Ireland is Scania's OmniExpress. This example, previously operated by Pat's Coaches, Southsea, Wrexham was acquired in May 2015 and re-registered with Select mark ER09 BUS in October.

*Left:* Most people in Belfast will be unaware of the daily express coach service operated by Patrick Gallagher, Brinalack, between northwest Co Donegal and Belfast. Seen on College Square North during its layover is Volvo B11R/Plaxton Panther 171 DL 2455, bought new in 2017.

*Below left:* Obviously impressed by the new Mercedes-Benz Tourismo it purchased earlier in the year, by 21 October 2017, Co Kerry-based Paddywagon had acquired a 2011 example, seen here crossing from Great Victoria Street to Fisherwick Place at the start of its run to the Giant's Causeway.

*Below right:* 24 November 2017, and its first full day in service in its new coat of overall magenta, Citybus (Metro) Volvo B7TL/Alexander Dennis ALX400 No 2975 leaves Donegall Square West, with the Scottish Provident building behind, as it heads for Knocknagoney to the east of the city. The painting of the ALX400 fleet was not expected, but rumour is that the Chief Executive didn't like the inconsistency of two livery schemes on double-deckers.

An interesting acquisition by Belfast City Sightseeing in November 2012 was 839 XUJ, a 1951 Leyland PS1, which had seen service previously on Jersey, Guernsey and in Edinburgh. For the 2013 Christmas period, it became a mobile Santa's Grotto, complete with exterior illuminations.

The yellow-liveried coaches of Chambers, Moneymore, were once a familiar sight throughout the United Kingdom and Ireland. The business has passed through a number of owners and the name now belongs to Glenshane Coach Hire of Maghera. V55 CCH, new in 2017, is an Irizar i6 integral, one of only two in Northern Ireland.

*Above:* Captured on Donegall Square North when brand new on 1 July 2014 was Metro Volvo B5TL/Wright Gemini 3 No 2392.

*Above right:* This anonymous vehicle actually belonged to Allen's Tours, Belfast, and when photographed, was setting off on a day tour to the Giant's Causeway via the Antrim Coast road, which is the core part of Allen's business. WXI 4418 is a Leyland Tiger with Wright Endeavour coachwork, new to Ulsterbus in 1992, but acquired at the auction of the assets of the Londonderry and Lough Swilly Railway Company in June 2014.

*Right:* Also new to Ulsterbus, but now in the fleet of Belfast City Sightseeing is MAN ND363F/Ayats Bravo 1 AXI 297, which had been No 2007 in the Ulsterbus fleet. New in June 2006, it was acquired by BCS ten years later.

*Above:* Belfast is now an important call on cruise ship itineraries and coaches from the very smart fleet of Logan, Dunloy, Co Antrim, can often be seen transporting visitors on tours of the city and beyond. On a damp 16 June 2016, Volvo B13RT/Plaxton Elite YX16 NWK collects visitors outside Belfast's tourist information centre.

*Left:* Perhaps the most luxurious schoolbuses in Northern Ireland are the eleven Volvo B9Rs in the Education Authority fleet. Eight of these 57-seat Plaxton Leopard-bodied coaches are based in the Authority's southern region, one in the south-eastern and two in the western. FXZ 6414 is one of those allocated to the southern region.

*Top left:* Giles Tours of Newtownards runs a small, but smart, fleet on private hire and holiday tours throughout the United Kingdom and Ireland. VDL Futura FHD2-122 SF15 BWE was new in July 2015, so was just weeks old when photographed passing City Hall on 9 September.

*Top right:* We've already had a look at the Halpenny Transport service bus fleet, at both Dundalk and Newry, but the company also operates a small fleet of modern, high quality coaches on private hire and contract tour operations. For the 2017 season, this Volvo B11R, with Jonckheere JHV2 coachwork, was purchased and put into service in April. It's seen here on 20 July.

*Left:* Allen's Tours Giant's Causeway day trip often loads to more than one coach, sometimes a full-size vehicle and a minibus, so when the opportunity arose to acquire a 79-seat coach, owner Benn Allen jumped at it. The vehicle in question, Volvo B10MA-55/ Van Hool Alizée DAZ 3001 was no stranger to Belfast as it was new to Citybus as its No 3001 before transferring to Ulsterbus and, later, acquisition by Morton's, Little London, Hants.

The oldest licensed operator in Northern Ireland is McAnulty's Yellow Line of Church Street, Warrenpoint, Co Down. Most of the vehicles in the fleet are elderly, but always well presented, Volvo B10M-62/Plaxton Premiere 350 YIL 7834, which dates from March 1998, being no exception as this October 2016 view shows.

In 1996, Ulsterbus acquired a batch of Mercedes-Benz 711D minibuses with Alexander AM bodies. On 4 August 2017, the former No 904, now with Michael Doonan, Derrylin, Co Fermanagh, was a surprise sighting on Donegall Square North. It reached Fermanagh in March 2016, when already twenty years old, after service with McGonagle, Buncrana, Co Donegal.

Based between Lisburn and Ballinderry, the smart coaches of the Richmond fleet can often be found in Belfast on hires, tours and work associated with visiting cruise ships. PBZ 2222 is a 2006 Scania K114EB/Irizar PB bought new.

Back in the summer of 2015, when warranty work was being undertaken on the fleet of Volvo B5TLs delivered to Metro, Volvo supplied on loan a similar vehicle as cover, it being allocated fleet number 2040. As it wasn't fitted with driver protection, had the glazed staircase panel and non-standard destination equipment, it was allocated to Ulsterbus at Newtownabbey depot, which happened to have an appropriate destination card from a vehicle received previously on demonstration.

The Belfast Rapid Transit network, now known as Glider, came into operation on 3 September 2018 and is operated with a fleet of 30 Van Hool Exqui.City hybrid-powered bendybuses. On 13/14 December 2017, shortly after it arrived in Belfast from Belgium, No 3201 was shown to the public at Custom House Square. Glider runs between Dundonald, in the east, and Dunmurry, in the west via the city centre. There will also be a branch between the city centre and Titanic Quarter.

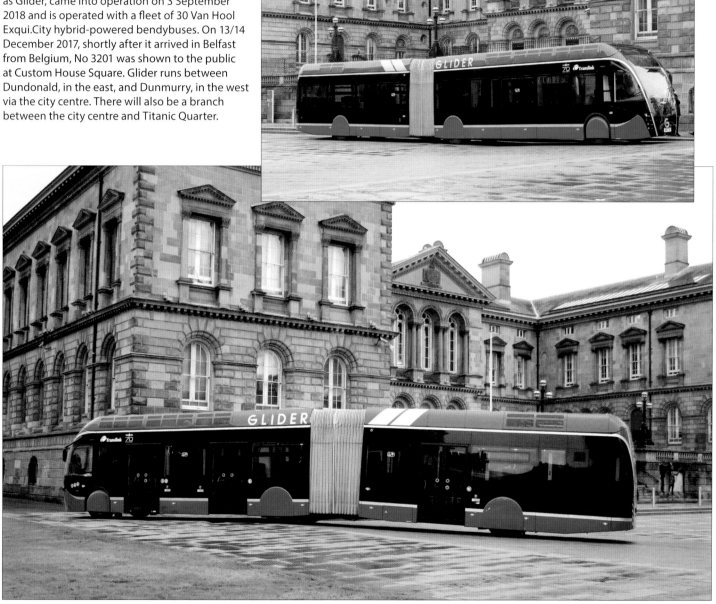

Seen on Queen Elizabeth Bridge not long after entering service is one of two Volvo B7TLs, with Wright Eclipse Gemini bodywork, in the Belfast City Sightseeing fleet. SFZ 7967, previously YK55 ATX, had worked for Yorkshire Coastliner before arrival in Belfast in March 2014 and conversion to part open-top layout.

*Above:* We cross to the Co Down side of the river for a June 2014 view of Metro Scania L94UB/Wright Solar No 702. New to Ulsterbus in March 2001, No 702 transferred to Metro in May 2009, was withdrawn in December 2015 and sold for scrap in November 2016.

*Left:* Diamond Leisure Transport trades as Titanic and City Tours and uses three ex-Dublin Bus Volvo B7TLs, two of which retain their roofs. The exception is RFZ 8427, previously 00 D 70125, Dublin Bus AV125. The dual door layout will be noticed, indicating that this one is from the small batch so built for use on the city centre to Dublin Airport route. It was acquired by Diamond in May 2013.

15:00, 11 June 2014 and Metro Volvo B5TL/Wright Gemini 3 No 2391 turns on the Titanic slipways just off Queen's Road, in the heart of the much redeveloped Titanic Quarter. No 2391 was being positioned for a photoshoot with representatives from Volvo, Wrightbus and Translink. Beyond, in the dry dock at the Harland & Wolff shipyard, is the Singapore-flagged deepwater drilling unit *Blackford Dolphin*.

Back across the river to Donegall Quay, once the departure point for the cross-channel ferries, but now regenerated with open spaces, public art and a footbridge and weir across the River Lagan. 2016 saw the first examples of the Macedonian-built Van Hool EX16H coach enter service in Ireland, with Cronin's of Cork whose Trafalgar-liveried example 161 C 10343 is seen heading for the Titanic Quarter on 8 August.

A surprise addition in December 2016 to the fleet of Allen's Tours was this Dennis Trident/Alexander ALX converted to part open-top layout for its previous owner, Golden Tours, London, whose livery it still wears. V204 MEV was new to Stagecoach London. Allen's left the Belfast sightseeing market in 2013.

In just about the same spot is another Dennis Trident, one of a pair acquired by Belfast City Sightseeing from Edinburgh Bus Tours in November 2016. V513 ESC carries Plaxton President bodywork.

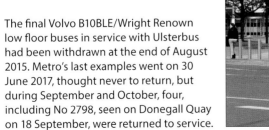

The final Volvo B10BLE/Wright Renown low floor buses in service with Ulsterbus had been withdrawn at the end of August 2015. Metro's last examples went on 30 June 2017, thought never to return, but during September and October, four, including No 2798, seen on Donegall Quay on 18 September, were returned to service.

August 2017 saw the two Metro Optare Versas allocated to the George Best Belfast City Airport service given a new blue livery to match the vehicles allocated to Ulsterbus service 300/a to Belfast International Airport; Versa No 1803 was similarly painted as spare. No 1802 was photographed at the Oxford Street bus gate on 15 August. This piece of traffic engineering is designed to assist buses coming off the Queen's Bridge to access the bus lane to May Street, which is lane 3 of Oxford Street. However, both bus gate and bus lane were removed in connection with works associated with the introduction of Glider in September 2018.

Cairns of Larne trades as Travelwise and operates a fleet of five coaches, which are always immaculately presented. This Scania K124IB/Van Hool T9 was new in April 2001 and was acquired by Cairns from Richmond, Lisburn, in 2010. In this July 2016 picture, it's seen on Oxford Street engaged on shuttle duties in connection with a major conference.

Coaches from several operators from the independent sector were contracted for this shuttle work, including Coach Connections Ireland (McDermott's of Portaferry) which provided VDL Futura FHD2-122 GCZ 5555, one of four in the fleet, all bought new.

Metro's fleet of Volvo B9TL/Wright Eclipse Gemini has been painted from magenta and grey to magenta allover, but only two similar Ulsterbus vehicles have received a like treatment, albeit in ocean blue, the first being No 2225, which was so painted in October 2016. At 15:30 on 27 February 2017 it's seen on the lower part of East Bridge Street passing St George's Market, near the end of its journey between Shrigley and Belfast's Laganside Bus Centre.

Ormeau Avenue now on an early spring day in 2014 and Ulsterbus Scania K94IB/Irizar Intercentury No 1750 heads for home at Downpatrick on the noon departure from Belfast's Europa Bus Centre. This limited stop journey on service 215 will take about three-quarters of an hour.

With Tyrone House, once government offices, but now apartments, to the right of the picture, Metro Volvo B7TL/Alexander ALX400 No 2935 leaves the city centre on the hourly service 77 to the southern suburbs around Newtownbreda, where the terminus is at a large Tesco store. No 2935 transferred to Ulsterbus in November 2014, about eight months after this view was taken and regularly passed this spot on its journeys from and to Cairnshill/Ballynahinch/Newcastle until it was stood down at the end of 2018.

Back now to the city centre, to Donegall Square and a view of East Coast Coaches of Newry Leyland Tiger DXI 3351, which had been new to Ulsterbus in June 1984, reaching East Coast in 2012 from an operator based at Dromara. This picture is dated 1 September 2014 and the Tiger carries its thirty years very well.

On 17 April 2017, Ulsterbus completed fifty years of service to the travelling public in Northern Ireland. After a little encouragement, the company agreed to paint a vehicle to an approximation of the Riviera Blue and Trader Ivory scheme applied to its first new buses delivered in 1967. The vehicle chosen was Scania K230UB/Wright Solar Rural No 551, which had recently been released from duties on service 300 to Belfast International Airport.

*Right:* Translink's schools safety education programme has been a great success and in September 2017 the vehicle used, Volvo B10BLE/ Wright Renown No 2785, was replaced with a newer Scania L94UB, No 2412, transferred from Ulsterbus, where it had been used on the park-and-ride service to Cairnshill.

*Below:* We return now to Donegall Square North and the start of our journey north from the city. Pictured leaving Donegall Place in this April 2017 view is Stranraer-allocated Scania K360EB/ Irizar i6 No 136, which, along with similar No 138, wears a broadside promotional advert for Scottish Citylink service 923; No 136 advertises Edinburgh, 138 Glasgow.

Eight months earlier and No 136 provides the odd sight of a National Express-liveried vehicle on Belfast's Royal Avenue. Nos 136–8 wore this livery for service 920 between Stranraer and London and service 921 between Stranraer and Birmingham. The latter service was withdrawn in June 2016 and the contract for the 920 lost from September.

2012 was a big year in the United Kingdom with London hosting the Olympic Games. As part of the celebrations, the Olympic torch toured the country and visited Belfast on 6 June. Included in the convoy, and in here because of its local connections, was Stagecoach No 43007, a Wright StreetLite WF destined for the South Wales fleet, seen here in north Belfast, crossing the Crumlin Road into Agnes Street.

The fleet renewal programme for Metro saw 23 more Volvo B5TLs delivered in 2017. Numbered 2100–32, they feature what has become known as the 'stealth' front, with glazed corner panels upstairs. Unlike the longer examples delivered to Ulsterbus, these do not feature glazed staircase panels. The last of the batch, No 2132, is shown here on the Shankill Road, looking towards Divis Mountain, with the television transmitters just visible.

Further north, we come to the junction of Alliance Avenue and Oldpark Road. The date is 30 June 2017 and Metro Volvo B10BLE/Wright Renown No 2850 is on one of its last journeys before withdrawal and sale to an operator in the Republic of Ireland. It had been new to Ulsterbus in March 2000 and reached Metro in September 2016.

## COUNTY ANTRIM

The next stop on our journey is Carrickfergus, on the northern shore of Belfast Lough. In November 2013, Belfast City Sightseeing purchased, from a preservationist, a Bristol MW5G with bodywork by Eastern Coach Works. Registered YBD 201, it dated from June 1961. One evening in August 2014, the management of Belfast City Sightseeing kindly made it available to a local enthusiasts' group for a trip along the Antrim Coast road, as shown here at Carrickfergus Castle.

Continuing along the A2 coast road we come to Larne, one of the main ferry ports, with frequent sailing to Cairnryan operated by P&O Irish Sea. The town has a reasonable network of town services, in addition to other local routes and the Goldline express service to Belfast. On 3 June 2017, Optare Solo M925SR No 1956 runs along Bridge Street towards Inver on the town service to the harbour.

On the same day, Scania L94UB/Wright Solar No 825 turns from Victoria Road into The Roddens as it heads out of town on the 14:35 service 130 departure to Ballymena, a journey of about three-quarters of an hour.

Via the A8, A57 and A6 now to Antrim and the integrated bus and rail station where, on 27 May 2017, Ballymena-allocated Volvo B7RLE/Alexander Dennis Enviro300 Rural No 542, new in April 2009, prepares to depart on the 14:35 service 120 to its home depot.

At Ballymena, four town service routes are operated, two of which run hourly Monday to Saturday, the others less frequently, particularly on Saturday. Here Ballymena depot's Scania L94UB/Wright Solar No 2436 has just passed under the Galgorm Road railway bridge, which carries the Belfast to Londonderry line, and is about to turn into the bus station.

Before we leave Ballymena, a visit to the showgrounds on 27 August 2016 allowed this picture of Volvo B10BLE/Wright Renown BCZ 2784 to be taken. This bus had been new to Citybus in October 1999, later passing to Ulsterbus before sale in April 2016 to the Dunglebe Sporting and Cultural Society, Ballymoney, which has had it painted to Transport for London red.

We've already seen several of the luxury coaches in the fleet of Logan, Dunloy, but many will be unaware of the town and local services operated around Ballymoney. These had operated since 1989, but changes to fuel duty rebate saw them withdrawn after Saturday 28 March 2015. About thirteen months earlier, Mellor-bodied Mercedes-Benz 614D UKZ 7139 (T364 BSS), new in May 1999 and acquired in March 2007, heads off on one of the two town services.

The local services were later upgraded with a pair of pre-owned Optare Solos – M850 model GRZ 7787 *(V115 DCF)* and M920 model GRZ 7789 *(V946 DCF, V111 DCF, V946 DCF)* which passed to Plaxton (dealer) on closure of the services. On 5 April 2014, GRZ 7789 leaves Ballymoney on the 11:30 departure to Garryduff Cross, Dunloy and Cloughmills.

# THE NORTH COAST

Ballycastle, famous for The Oul' Lammas Fair at the end of August each year, is our next port of call. Indeed, Ballycastle is a port, with car and passenger ferry services to Rathlin Island all year round and summer seasonal fast craft services to Campbeltown and Port Ellen. Ulsterbus No 605, seen arriving at the Marine Corner departure point to take up the 12:45 service 131 to Ballymena on 9 September 2017, is a Scania K320IB/Irizar i4 55-seater new in June 2013.

*Right:* Having just left the Marine Corner stop on 17 June 2017, Volvo B7RLE/Alexander Dennis Enviro300 Rural No 526 will shortly call at the town centre stop at the Anzac Bar before heading for the A44 towards Armoy and Killagan en route to Ballymena.

*Below:* We now reach Northern Ireland's most popular visitor attraction, the Giant's Causeway, just a couple of miles from Bushmills with its world famous distillery. The Logan coaching fleet is replaced every three years and in this July 2015 view we see Volvo B8R/Plaxton Panther Cub MX15 KLD, then just over two months old. Logan's operates tours on contract to several companies, including CIÉ Tours International.

*Left:* The expansion of the motorway network in the Republic of Ireland and the upgrading of the A26 to dual-carriageway to beyond Killagan, north of Ballymena, means that Dublin-based operators can offer day trips as far north as the Causeway. One is Extreme Event Ireland, which for the 2017 season bought three of these Macedonian-built Van Hool EX15H coaches. This is 171 D 40888 leaving for home on 29 July 2017.

*Below:* Three weeks previously and with the beach at Whiterocks in the background, Ulsterbus Volvo B7RLE/Alexander Dennis Enviro300 Rural No 512, then working from the outstation at Ballycastle, departs the Causeway stop by The Nook and heads for Dunseverick and Ballycastle on service 172.

*Right:* Prior to the 2017 summer timetable, there were just two Saturday journeys between the Giant's Causeway and Ballycastle, but, between June and September that was increased to half-hourly, with the extension of service 402 beyond Carrick-a-Rede rope bridge. One such journey in July was worked by Scania L94UB/Wright Solar No 711, new in May 2001.

*Below:* Parking at the Causeway site can be a problem and the National Trust has contracted PK Travel, of Whitepark Road, Ballycastle to provide a park-and-ride service based at Dundarave, Bushmills. Two Optare Solos are operated, one of which is M880SL model NHZ 6321, new in January 2008 to the associated Keogh, Clarecastle, Co Clare fleet as 08 CE 444.

Ulsterbus service 477 operates along the single-track road between the visitor centre and the Causeway. The usual vehicles are Plaxton Primos Nos 3 and 4, which date from 2007 and acquired in 2009, but for 2017 a third vehicle, Optare Solo M850SL No 1929, was painted in the special green livery and waits, with No 3, for its next load of visitors.

On a sunny 25 July 2015, Plaxton Primo No 4 returns from the Causeway, to the left in this view, fully laden with another crowd of visitors. The registration numbers carried by Nos 3 and 4 were transferred from Leyland Tigers Nos 1333 and 1400 in 2010.

*Left:* A year earlier and Matthews, Inniskeen, Co Monaghan, Volvo B11R/Plaxton Elite i 141 MN 219, then just a few months old, arrives to pick-up its party of students. The Elite i features a wide entrance, with space for a wheelchair on the platform and just four seats downstairs.

*Below:* Arriving at The Nook, at the entrance to the Giant's Causeway site on 22 July 2017, is Ulsterbus No 119, a 2006 Volvo B12M with Plaxton Panther coachwork. No 119 was the last Volvo coach purchased by Ulsterbus for touring duties, though four B12B models arrived towards the year's end for use on the cross-channel express network.

Also arriving from the Dunseverick direction, after a visit to the rope bridge at Carrick-a-Rede, is Paddywagon's Scania K400EB6/Irizar i6 131 KY 221, new in 2013. Paddywagon is based at Annascaul, Co Kerry and specialises in transport and hostels for backpackers, though day tours are now an important part of its activities. Indeed, this tour is likely to have started from Dublin. The coach was withdrawn in the Autumn of 2017 and sold to Corduff, Rossport, Co Mayo.

*Below left:* We continue our journey along the coast towards Portrush, the A2 coast road running along the cliffs for much of the way. Near Dunluce Castle on 4 August 2012, Scania N113CRB/Van Hool Alizée 96 DL 5683 from the fleet of Reddin, Muff, Co Donegal, passes by. It was new in September 1996 to Bournemouth Transport (for National Express duties) as N368 TJT and passed to the Birmingham Coach Company before reaching Co Donegal. It has since transferred to the Northern Ireland branch of the Reddin company and been registered TUI 8531.

*Below right:* The seaside town of Portrush is popular with holidaymakers and day trippers; May and June see a lot of Sunday school excursions. 28 June 2014 saw Volvo B10M-62/Plaxton Premiere 320 DAZ 1565 on such an outing. Then in the fleet of Davison, Dungannon, it had been new in July 1994 as Ulsterbus No 1565, Davison acquiring it from Easter Ross, Tain, in July 2012. It has since been withdrawn.

The north coast has two world-class golf courses, at Portrush and Portstewart. Royal Portrush is to host the British Open in 2019, but, in 2017, Portstewart had the honour of hosting the Irish Open. For the event, Ulsterbus Volvo B9TL/Wright Eclipse Gemini No 2264 was given a vinyl wrap promoting golf on the north coast. Here it's approaching Portstewart golf club on 8 July on one of the park-and-ride shuttles.

For 2017, several journeys daily on Ulsterbus service 402 were noted as being operated by the part open-top former Dublin Bus Volvo Olympian No 2000. However, for various reasons, appearances were few and far between. Indeed, the only occasion that summer on which I saw it moving was on a shuttle service at the Portstewart golf club.

# DERRY CITY AND LETTERKENNY

From Coleraine, we follow the A37 and A2 roads towards our next port of call, Derry or Londonderry depending on your preference, or The Maiden City, maiden because the walls which surround it were never breached. On the outskirts of the city, at Gransha, is a large health and social care facility where, on 18 November 2017, Reddin's Dennis Trident/Alexander ALX400 V215 MEV, fleetnumber DT1, was engaged on a shuttle service to the city centre in connection with an athletics event taking place in the grounds. DT1 had previously worked for Stagecoach London as its No 17215 and reached Northern Ireland in April 2012.

On the second Saturday in August each year, the Apprentice Boys of Derry, one of the Loyal Orders, holds a major demonstration marking the relief of the city following the 1689 siege. This requires a major coaching operation, which in 2016 included Ulsterbus No 1681, an Irizar Intercentury-bodied Scania K94IB allocated to Ballymena depot. Unfortunately, on 2 June 2017, No 1681 was severely damaged by an engine fire at Knockstacken, when running empty from St Killian's College, Garron Tower; it was withdrawn and sold for scrap.

The Ulsterbus contribution to this event has reduced over the years, much work now being undertaken by the private sector. In 2016, Causeway, Ballymoney, had turned out its smart Dennis R410/Plaxton, seen here resting by the Caw Camp on the Clooney Road.

Eurocoach, Dungannon Volvo B10M-62/Plaxton Excalibur BCZ 1657 was photographed at the 2015 Relief of Derry event. It was acquired from Ulsterbus in 2013 and re-seated C70F. It was certainly on familiar ground as it had spent its entire Ulsterbus service allocated to Londonderry, latterly as a depot tours coach.

The scale of the operation may be illustrated with this view looking along Victoria Road towards the city centre. The front vehicle is a Leyland Tiger, with Wright Endeavour coachwork and was new in 1992 as Ulsterbus Goldliner No 1415. It now belongs to Charlie McGowan, Strabane, who acquired it at the auction of the assets of the Londonderry and Lough Swilly Railway Company in June 2014. It had been numbered 529 in that fleet.

We head back towards the city now and cross from the Waterside to the Cityside on the Craigavon Bridge where Ulsterbus Goldliner No 1780, a Volvo B12B/Sunsundegui Sideral new in April 2008, nears journey's end at Foyle Street Bus Centre on the 11:45 service 273 departure from Belfast via Omagh.

A few yards further on, on 2 September 2017, and we get our first glimpse of the 'burnt orange' colour and Foyle Metro brand introduced to the city services officially from the previous day. Ulsterbus No 1825 is an Optare Versa V1170, new as part of the 2017 renewal programme. Oddly, the licensing authority at Swansea allocated numbers which were two-and-a-half years old, but at least they matched the fleetnumbers.

On the opposite side of John Street roundabout, and four years later, Ulsterbus Scania K230IB4/Irizar i4 No 1018, new in July 2012, departs the city on a service 273 journey to Belfast via Strabane, Omagh and Dungannon. These 51-seat vehicles have leather seats and a side-mounted wheelchair lift fitted amidships.

*Above left:* To complete the Foyle Metro allocation of full-size single-deck buses, seven Scania L94UBs, Nos 841–7 were also given a coat of 'burnt orange'. Here No 843 runs from Carlisle Road towards the Craigavon Bridge on a 4c journey to Currynierin. Similar No 830 was a further addition to the 'burnt orange' fleet, in November 2017.

*Above right:* For several summers prior to pulling off the route completely, Bus Éireann operated a twice daily, X33 from Dublin and Dublin Airport non-stop to Derry. The operation in 2013 was contracted to Boyce, Ramelton, who used this appropriately-vinylled new Neoplan Tourliner. Here, on 17 August 2013, 131 DL 1359 rounds John Street roundabout, with just a few hundred yards to go to its destination. The X33 wasn't included in the joint operation with Ulsterbus of the Derry/Dublin route.

The city's tourist information centre is located on Foyle Street where the city tour operated by CitySightseeing franchisee Wray, Londonderry, begins. Volvo Olympian UUI 3685, acquired in 2013, was Dublin Bus RV555 (99 D 10555) in its previous life.

*Left:* With its smart turnout belying its age, Belfast Bus Company's PFZ 7768, a Volvo B10M-62 with Caetano Enigma coachwork new in July 2001 and acquired in October 2013, heads towards Foyle Road and the lower deck of the Craigavon Bridge. It was new to Bus Éireann as its fleet number VC 210, registered 01 D 66557.

*Below:* The introduction of new Optare Versa V1170 buses at Craigavon in April 2017 saw the displacement of older Wright Solar-bodied Scania L94UBs to other depots. Several went to the Foyle allocation, including No 767 seen on the Harbour Square roundabout on 12 August. The observant reader will note that it was then still carrying promotional material for a special fare between Lurgan and Portadown. No doubt the citizens of Derry~Londonderry found that most helpful!

*Above:* The Foyle Metro fleetname first appeared on Volvo B9TL/Wright Eclipse Gemini No 2240, which featured images of three local 'legends' selected by the general public. It's seen here turning from Eden Terrace on to Northland Road. The wrap was removed in autumn 2018 and No 2240 became the second of its type to appear in allover ocean blue.

*Right:* One of the oldest buses working at Foyle in 2017 was Volvo B7TL No 2937, which dated from June 2001, when it was new to Citybus in Belfast. It reached Derry in September 2015 and is seen here two months later loading on Foyle Street for a run to Shantallow. The bodywork on No 2937 was built at the since-closed Mallusk factory of Walter Alexander.

*Top:* The most popular buses with city service drivers were the Volvo B10BLEs with Wright Renown bodywork, such as No 2839 seen on Foyle Street on 8 March 2014. The last examples were withdrawn on 31 August 2015 after fifteen-and-a-half years service.

*Below left:* With the knowledge that sixteen Optare Versa V1170s would be taking up service on the Foyle Metro network later in the year, in April three blue examples, which had been provisionally allocated to Ballymena, took up service at Derry to ensure they were suitable for all routes. Here No 1821 is turning from Ardan Road to the stop at Culmore Point, on the west bank of the Foyle.

*Below right:* June 2017 gave the citizens of Londonderry the first sight of the 'burnt orange' Foyle Metro livery when three new Optare Solo M925SR midibuses, numbered 1971–3, entered service on city routes. No 1971 is seen on the Foyle Embankment heading for Foyle Street to start its run on service FY8 to the Creggan estate.

*Left:* The assets of the Londonderry and Lough Swilly Railway Company, which had closed in April, were sold at auction on Saturday 14 June 2014. A couple of days prior, a line-up of 12 Alexander Q-type and Wright Endeavour Leyland Tigers is seen at the Springtown premises.

*Below:* The final vehicles were removed by their new owners on 18 June. Dennis Dart No 503 raises a cloud of dust as it speeds away from Springtown on its final journey. It would be scrapped by Hamill, at Ahoghill, just a few miles from where the Handybus body was built by Wrights at Galgorm. No 503 had been numbered 630 in the Citybus fleet and had been acquired by the Swilly in April 2006.

At 17:18 on Wednesday 18 June 2014, Dennis Dart No 501, previously Citybus No 637, became the final Lough Swilly bus to leave the Springtown site. It had been purchased, with others, for breaking, by Aidan Caldwell, Strabane. However, it was unwilling to go and it took several hours of 'encouragement' by the former Swilly foreman, Gerry Storey, before it would move.

Northwest Busways had been competing over Lough Swilly routes since September 1992, though taken over in May 2000 by the current owner, Joe McGonagle, already a well-established operator in the area, on the retirement of the original directors. In Derry, services depart from the Patrick Street stand once used by Lough Swilly services. Here, on 22 November 2014, Volvo B10M/Plaxton Premiere 350 96 D 42490 awaits customers for Moville and Carndonagh. This coach had previously operated for Bus Éireann as its VP 32.

On Queen's Quay, Derry on 23 July 2016, Mercedes-Benz 1223L/Euro 03 OY 1150 arrives from Carndonagh followed by 05 DL 12494, a Marcopolo-bodied MAN 18.310 previously in the service of the UK Ministry of Defence.

Within days of the Lough Swilly closure in April 2014, McGonagle's of Buncrana had been granted a temporary licence to operate the Buncrana to Derry route. Initially, coaches from the main fleet were used, but suitable service buses have been bought since, the latest being a pair of Optare Versa V1100, last with the now defunct Webberbus of Bridgewater, Somerset. Here 10 DL 14444 runs on to the Harbour Square roundabout on 12 August 2017. The number 956 affixed to the destination glass is the route number.

*Above left:* Other vehicles used on the service have included a pair of former Dublin Bus Volvo B6BLE/Wright, which still wear their previous owner's livery. This one, on the stop at Whittaker Street, beside Derry's Guildhall, was WV43 in the Dublin Bus fleet.

*Above right:* Several Optare Solos previously in the Citybus and Ulsterbus fleets were also acquired. M850 model 03 DL 11903 had been No 1863 in the Ulsterbus fleet and was acquired in 2014. On 23 May 2015, it's seen arriving at Whittaker Street to operate the 15:10 to Buncrana via Bridgend, Burnfoot and Fahan.

*Right:* Our final view in Derry of an Ulsterbus vehicle is of No 2287, one of nine Volvo B9TL/Wright Eclipse Gemini double-deckers to receive Foyle Metro colours. With the Guildhall behind, it's approaching the junction of Whittaker Street and Foyle Embankment, a few hundred metres into its journey on service 12a to Slievemore, despite what it says on the front!

13 May 2017 and twelve-year-old Bus Éireann Scania K114EB/Irizar PB SP 22 leaves Foyle Street Bus Centre, Derry, on an *Expressway* 64 short journey to Letterkenny. The through service from Derry extends beyond Letterkenny to Donegal, Sligo and, ultimately, Galway.

Then almost nineteen-years-old – it was new in June 1997 – Volvo B10M-62/Caetano Algarve VC 105 rests on the lay-bys at Foyle Street between runs to Letterkenny on 14 May 2016.

28 January 2017 saw Scania K114IB/Irizar Century SC 52 allocated to the noon service 480 between Derry and Donegal Town. It's seen here on the Foyle Embankment heading for Foyle Road and Letterkenny. SC52 was new in March 2004 and, despite some grime from the winter roads, looks smart on a sunny, winter day.

*Top left:* We depart Derry for Letterkenny with this August 2013 view at John Street roundabout of Bus Éireann Scania K114EB/Irizar PB SP 90, one of two tri-axle models delivered in July 2006 for use on Eurolines service 890 from Cork and Waterford to London. Here it wears a scheme specially applied to promote The Gathering 2013, a programme of events designed to encourage ex-pats to return to Ireland for a visit. On arrival in Dublin, SP 90 would likely have been used on Eurolines service 880 to Leeds, but only as far as the Holyhead ferry.

*Top right:* At Letterkenny on 3 October 2015 is Mangan, Gortahork Volvo B10M-62/Plaxton Excalibur 99 DL 11442 awaiting departure on the 13:00 service to Falcarragh and Crolly. The livery might be a giveaway! This vehicle was previously No 1632 in the Ulsterbus fleet and was one of several similar vehicles sold by Ulsterbus to Carolan, Nobber, Co Meath. It has been in the fleet of JMB Tours, Cookstown, Co Tyrone since August 2016.

*Left:* Branded for route 20 Galway to Dublin, Bus Éireann Scania K114EB/Irizar PB SP 70 puts in an appearance on route 64 Galway to Derry on the same day. After rounding the station roundabout, SP 70 would enter the bus station, on the site of the former County Donegal Railways terminus.

# TYRONE, FERMANAGH AND ARMAGH

Bus Éireann Scania K340EB/Irizar Century SC 234 was new in April 2008 and has spent its service so far on local services operated from the garage at Stranorlar. Here, on 3 December 2016, it heads out of Strabane on local route 487 to Letterkenny via Ballindrait, Raphoe and Convoy. It's a 55-seater with a side-mounted wheelchair lift.

In addition to the Ulsterbus-operated Derry~Londonderry to Dublin *Goldline* X3 service, passengers at Strabane, Omagh, Ballygawley and Aughnacloy can also avail of Bus Éireann *Expressway* route 32, on which several journeys are operated with VDL Synergy double-deck coaches such as Stranorlar-allocated LE 8, shown leaving Strabane for Letterkenny on 3 December 2016.

13:20 on 3 December 2016 and Ulsterbus MAN ND363F/Ayats Bravo 1 double-deck coach No 2021 has arrived with the 12:50 service 273 from Derry~Londonderry to Belfast via Omagh and Dungannon. It will reach its destination at 15:45 and return to Derry via the same route at 16:45.

*Top left:* A brief visit to Omagh now, on 31 August 2012, for a view of Bus Éireann VDL Synergy LE 4 departing on route 32 for Letterkenny. At this date, LE 4, normally to be found on route 1 between Dublin and Belfast, was just about three months old.

*Top right:* Moving on to Co Fermanagh now and the county town of Enniskillen and the arrival on 9 April 2016 of Ulsterbus Scania K230UB/Wright Solar Rural No 463, an Omagh bus. Wrights designed the Solar Rural to an Ulsterbus specification with a narrower entrance, 55 seats (in a mix of 2+2 and 3+2 layout) and with wheelchair access via a door located just behind the front axle.

*Left:* Enniskillen is served by Bus Éireann routes 458 from Ballina and 30 between Dublin and Donegal Town, also on Thursdays only 464 from Carrigallen. On 31 October 2015, Irizar i6-bodied Scania K410 SE 29 arrives from Donegal Town to be the 12:05 route 30 to Dublin Airport and Dublin city centre via Cavan. SE 29 was one of a number of similar coaches given all-over schemes in 2015 celebrating Irish design. The idea of travelling a long distance on a coach with its windows covered in Contravision certainly wouldn't be one which appeals, though.

Bus Éireann route 458 was created in March 2016 by combining the Ballina to Sligo and Sligo to Enniskillen services into a through route operating up to three through journeys Monday to Saturday, two on Sundays. Shortly after the route's introduction, Scania K310/Irizar Century SC 249 heads away from Enniskillen with the 14:15 departure for Ballina, where it was scheduled to arrive at 17:30.

In 2013, following cutbacks by Bus Éireann, Leydon's Coaches of Swanlinbar, Co Cavan, introduced route 930 between Cavan and Enniskillen via west Co Cavan towns and villages. This unusual, short Optare Excel, new to Stockton Council, was acquired for the service and is seen here on 23 November 2013 by Enniskillen bus station en route to the Erneside shopping centre.

*Left:* Route 930 still operates in 2017, but the section between Swanlinbar and Enniskillen now operates only on Tuesdays and Saturdays. The usual vehicle, which entered service in September 2017, is Optare Solo M920SL 05 CN 6472, which began life as Ulsterbus No 1891, though Leydon's acquired it from Coyle, Ardara, Co Donegal.

*Below left:* On 29 October 2016, the 14:10 service 94 departure from Enniskillen to Omagh was worked with Volvo B7R/Wright SchoolRun No 308. There are 220 similar vehicles in the Ulsterbus fleet, with seating capacities of between 62 and 66, depending on the seating layout, most of which is in 3+2 format for use on schools services.

*Below right:* With the spires of St Michael's church (left of picture) and St Macartin's Cathedral (right) beyond, Optare Solo M920SL No 1875 runs along Shore Road, on its approach to the bus station, while undertaking a turn on the town service on 9 April 2016.

At Dungannon, the bus station and garage share a site at Beech Valley, not far from the site of the long-closed railway station. Outside the garage on 15 March 2014 are Volvo B7TL/Alexander Dennis No 2316, Volvo B7R/Wright SchoolRun No 222, Volvo B7R/Wright High Capacity No 386 and MAN ND363F/Ayats Bravo 1 No 2004. Note, too, the Ulsterbus name on the garage is displayed in the italicised Roman style introduced in 1967!

The same day, passengers at Dungannon Square board Volvo B7RLE/Alexander Dennis Enviro300 Rural No 518 for Cookstown via Coalisland and Stewartstown. Most local services still call at the Square, but *Goldline* services operate direct from the bus station to the motorway or A4 dual carriageway.

Down the A29 to the cathedral city of Armagh and a view of The Mall, with Volvo B9TL/Wright Eclipse Gemini No 2270 heading off on the 13:15 service 40 to Markethill, Mountnorris and Newry on 20 May 2017.

At the stops further along The Mall, Scania K230UB/Wright Solar Rural No 564 is on one of the city service routes, while Scania L94UB/Wright Solar No 2417 loads for Tassagh and Keady.

The area between the towns of Portadown and Lurgan is known as Craigavon, named after Northern Ireland's first Prime Minister, James Craig, 1st Viscount Craigavon. Intended to be a new linear city, the plan was abandoned and less than half of the proposed work was completed. The central area is known as Highfield and incorporates the council offices, courts and a large shopping centre, Rushmere, where Optare Versa V1170 No 1813, which entered service at Craigavon depot on 11 April 2017, is seen departing for Lurgan to take up a run to Banbridge. The Lurgan to Banbridge service was taken over with the closure of Sureline Coaches, Lurgan in June 1987.

New in September 2006, Scania L94UB/Wright Solar No 2425 rests on the Market Square at Lurgan having just arrived on a service 47 journey from Portadown via Highfield and Rushmere. The registration number, FXI 385, was previously carried on a Leyland Tiger.

We end our tour at Lisburn. The Royal Ulster Agricultural Society show, previously held in Belfast, at Balmoral, now takes place each May at the redeveloped Balmoral Park site, outside Lisburn. This requires a major bus shuttle service from the railway station, with vehicles and drivers drafted in from across the province. On 14 May 2015, Citybus Volvo B7TL/Alexander ALX400 No 2929, wearing promotional vinyls for Smartlink tickets, heads for the show.